Your Guide To A Successful Black Owned Business

D. Brandon Campbell

Printed in the United States of America

First Printing, 2020

Christianpreneur Publishing

ChristianpreneurCo@gmail.com

Table of Contents:

Introduction

Hey there! I want to start this book by saying, thank you for purchasing your copy of *Your Guide To A Successful Black Owned Business*. Whew! Long name, right? I know it is just the right name, though, because I wanted you to be aware from just a glance (be it a long glance) at the cover, precisely the purpose of this book. This book is to help black-owned businesses be successful.

Now let me go ahead and address this quickly. Does my book title mean I don't want businesses owned by other races to be successful? Of course not. I want success for anybody willing to work hard for it and will use it for good. But I see a need in my community, and I want to help meet that need. Since black people are growing by leaps and bounds in the "starting small businesses" category, I think it's time that someone in our community tells us how to do this thing right. I don't have all the answers, but I'd like to share a few.

This book's basis is my observations as a customer, black business owner, consultant, and employee in customer service. I've had to handle customers from a management standpoint, an owner's standpoint, and a trainer's standpoint. I've been treated terribly by businesses, and sometimes I've not been the best customer. I've been on three sides of the equation as a customer, owner, manager—so I figured I had something of value to offer you, black business owners.

Meet a Need

Let me go ahead and offer you some of that value right here in the introduction; meeting a need is the number one way to become successful with your black-owned business. Having a niche or novelty product is excellent, but if you have a product or service that meets a need, you will see success much faster and easier. Ask yourself, what demand does your current business, service, or business idea meet? If you can answer that question, then you'll know how to do your marketing, and your marketing is the key that opens the door to your success.

You've already gotten something of value from this book, and you're just in the first couple of pages of the introduction! That's awesome. Now, I will spend the next few paragraphs telling you a little about me and why I wrote this book. You're going to want to read this introduction because it will tell you why I'm qualified to give you this advice. Hint, it's not because I'm so educated or run a multi-billion dollar enterprise (not yet, at least).

About Me

As I'm sure you've already figured out from the cover, my name is D. Brandon Campbell. No, I will NOT tell you what the 'D' stands for, so do not ask me. I am in the older category of Millennials.

And trust me, there's a difference between early to mid 80's babies who are Millennials and late 80's to 90's babies who are also considered millennials. We are a different breed, us older "Mills." We tend to benefit from being a Millennial while carrying the weight of our parent's issues. We are the big brothers and sisters who watched our parents give our younger siblings freedoms we couldn't even imagine. Our parents practiced on us and changed after us. We saw their faults and adopted a few of them as our own. We're a complicated yet very essential component of society.

I am a single father that had a baby at 19 years old with an amazing girl that I was not ready or mature enough to keep, hence me being single. My one and only little dude, as I call him, is named

Trevon. Because I had him early, I am in my mid 30's, and he is a year from going to college! Part of me is ecstatic, and part of me feels old, very old. But that's how the cookie crumbles (whatever that means). He's also my favorite son.

Paperboy Chronicles

I got my first job at ten years old. Yeah, you read that right. I got a position with a newspaper in Elgin, Illinois as a paperboy. My boss interviewed me for the role after I walked into the newspaper because I saw the sign outside that said, "Paperboy Wanted." He talked to me for 20 minutes and offered me the job on the spot. I was so happy. He then asked me for my State ID or high school ID, and of course, at ten years old, I had neither. I said to him that *Channing*, my elementary school, did not issue IDs to us. His eyes got big, and he said, “wait, what? How old are you?” I replied, thinking he had to know I was a kid, “10.” He sank into his chair and said, “I can’t hire a 10-year-old.” I sat up in my chair and said, “why not?” A minute ago, you offered me the job, and now I can’t have it?” He looked at me and told me not to tell anyone else my age. From this point on, I was 14, in high school, and on a work permit. I didn’t even know what that was at the time, but okay, I got a job.

I got the job without my mom knowing. She would work after I got out of school until about 6p, so I just started working and didn’t tell her anything until I got my first check. I had to let her know because I had no idea how to cash a check as a 10-year-old. I told mom to take $60 of my $80 of pay (for two weeks of work), leaving me with $20 (this was big money for a 10-year-old in the '90s). She was in tears as I told her that I wanted to help with the bills around the house and I wasn't doing anything after school but a little homework, so I could deliver some papers for 2 hours and make some money to help out. All she said was, "you are something else."

I got 2 or 3 checks at the rate of $80, and I didn't think it was enough. I want $40 for myself and to give my mom $80. So I needed to make at least $120 every two weeks. I went to my boss and asked him how I was doing. He said I was one of the best paperboys they had at the *Daily Courier* (I just remembered the name when I typed it). I was thrilled to hear that because, after six weeks of working there, I told him, “I’d now like a raise.” He laughed at me and called me ambitious. That was great, but sir, how do I get this money? I have a goal to give me and my mama both a $20 raise. He told me that if I wanted more money, I needed to get more clients on my route. He told me to knock on doors and talk to people to join the paper’s subscription list. So I grabbed a stack of flyers and hit the streets. Every day after school, I waved at people on the way home and handed leaflets to anyone walking by. I told the ones that would talk to me that I wanted to help my mama, so I need more customers.

Within a two week timeframe, I more than doubled my customer count. I had 18 clients that I delivered papers to six days a week. I got my client list up to 27 customers. Then I started ringing bells of old and new customers, asking if they needed anything. I introduced myself. I asked them questions like, did they want their paper in a specific spot? I wrote down the ones that made requests and did what they asked. They then began giving me tips. Now, I make more money from having a more massive client list, and I make occasional tips. I kept the tips to myself; mama wasn't getting those. But she got her $80!

One lady, in particular, was known as a "meanie" to her neighbors. Her next-door neighbor told me not to knock on her door because she would never answer. So, of course, I did what entrepreneurs do; I went against the grain. I knocked on her door for three days straight. On the third day, she arose. She answered the door. I was scared as can be! I gave her my speech through the door and asked if she needed anything or had a preference for her paper's location. She said no one has ever even asked her that before. I told her, "I figured since you don't come out much that maybe you'd want your paper inside the screen door, so you don't have to come out to get it. After a little pause, she verbally agreed through the wood door. And from that point on, every Sunday, she left me an envelope full of loose change as a tip. One time it was over $30 in the envelope! She even bought me a Christmas gift in addition to the money she gave me.

What I Learned

Hear me; you may think that I'm just having a moment of nostalgia, but I am telling you this story because it was the birthplace of my entrepreneurial spirit. I wasn't satisfied with my pay, so I learned marketing and networking skills to take my paycheck from $80 every two weeks to $140 every two weeks. I also learned how to pitch my product by talking to people, waving at cars, and handing out flyers. At 10, I wasn't worried about being told no or whether they would buy my paper or not. I focused on the goal. I wanted more money, my boss said to get more customers, so I did. Not only did I get more customers for my route, but I got more for two other routes too. They were out of my district, so, unfortunately, I couldn't have them, but that's okay. Somebody else in my newspaper got blessed from my hard work. If you're reading, you're welcome.

I couldn't control the price of the paper. I couldn't control the content inside the newspaper. But what I could control is the service I offered (customer service) delivering the paper. I could ask them where they wanted their paper (problem-solving). I could hand a flyer to anyone walking by (networking). I could wave at cars with my newspaper bag facing the traffic (marketing). I couldn't control how much the paper would give me per customer (overhead), but I knew that if I was going to make more money (profit margins), I had to have more customers (supply & demand).

My First Business

I started my first business at 12. I hand-made 100 flyers and walked them to 100 doors in my neighborhood. I had this great business idea. I live in Chicago, and it snows like crazy in the winter. People hated shoveling snow, so I was going to be their snow shoveler. I got two friends together and started my own snow shoveling business. In the Fall, we would expand to raking leaves, cutting grass in the spring & summer. We never got that far, though. My employees bailed on me after just two jobs, and in Chicago, where it snows about 25 times a winter, it only snowed seven times that year. I made a killing on the first snow, but I would only have 1 or 2 jobs a week after that. After the winter ended that year, I let the business go. To my two friends that bailed on me, you all still suck. Love you, though.

I started my community choir (one not based out of a particular church) at 17. We sang all over the city of Chicago for years. I started a Church at 26. I founded my first digital company at 29. I opened my first brick and mortar business at 31. I wrote my first bestseller at 34. I wrote the second bestseller at 35. This book will be the 3rd one; I'm 36.

I've worked with and for multi-billion dollar corporations in their customer service departments, profit and loss statement creation, merchandising, and more. The companies I've worked with include La-Z-Boy, Starbucks & Walmart. I've been to their warehouses and distribution centers. I've trained hundreds of their employees and have been to dozens of their stores. I've held diversity workshops for them, organized community campaigns alongside them, and have helped them with emergency response efforts when there were natural disasters.

What I Do Now

I am now the founder and CEO of the Christianpreneur Company that houses Churchismtees.com, hAPPyAppsBuilder.com,

OfficialBlackApp.com, The Devoinaire Collection, Black CEO Brand & Black CEO Magazine. We are a profitable company because we have low overhead, great products at great prices, and oh, that son that I told you about earlier? I made him a part-owner. When he writes his book, it can say that he became part owner of a company at 17. He also started his business selling products at age 14. I guess it runs in the family. Please support my little dude and purchase some Devoinaire Collection products on OfficialBlackApp.com.

Why Did I Write This Book?

I am writing this book because I know what makes a multi-billion dollar corporation tick on the service level. I know their ins and outs. I saw their weaknesses. Companies hire me to help fix those weaknesses in their stores, employees, and in some cases, in their entire district of stores. I've had to work with HR departments in each company. I've had to fix customer service standards in their companies, and guess what? All of that impresses some people, but the real reason I am qualified to write this book is that I am still a student. I am still learning and will continue to learn for the rest of my life. But for now, I've learned enough to help others along the way. So let me drop some of this knowledge. I believe in putting others on when I've been put on. I believe in looking out for others when others have looked out for me.

My community needs what I'm writing in this book. Why? Because I believe that someone is reading, maybe you will be the next Sam Walton (Walmart). Perhaps you're the next Ed Knabusch that founded La-Z-Boy. Or possibly you are the next Howard Schultz. But even if you never achieve that level of success with your business, it is perfectly fine being the next you. The next you, is the you, that you will be after you read this book.

You know a bit about me, now tell me a little about you—post on social media a little about your journey using the hashtag #MyBlackOwnedBusinessJourney. Who knows, maybe you will inspire someone, and just perhaps, you'll see a reply from me.

Let's dive in.

Chapter

1

Hustler vs. Entrepreneur

Chapter 1:

Hustler vs. Entrepreneur

Let me just burst out the gate saying that I hate when entrepreneurs refer to themselves as hustlers. I know it sounds cool to say you're on your hustle. But it's this kind of phrasing that shapes how we and others view our business. There is a difference between a hustler and an entrepreneur. I'll spend the next chapter ranting about why you should not call yourself a hustler but an entrepreneur. But let me first tell you how I learned the difference between the 2.

In my early 20's I got suckered into working for a "marketing firm" that was just a cover for a bootleg cologne selling operation. I remember the boss was this well-dressed lady who reminded me of Meryl Streep's character on *The Devil Wears Prada*. Her office was in a great part of town, and she knew how to run her operation. Like clockwork, she had mounds of people coming in to work for her in this business. This whole operation, though, was a complete hustle. She got mad one day and went off. She said, "I don't need a bunch of pansies on my team! I need some got-damn hustlers!" I thought to myself, "oh well, that's not me. I don't hustle." So I left the company after just a couple of weeks. I'm surprised I even stayed that long, but I tried to justify being there every day.

She wanted hustlers because she was running a hustle. When she said it, I knew exactly what she meant because the trainer assigned to me was willing to sleep with me for motivation to do the job well. She flat out told me in the most matter-of-fact kind of way that she would give me “some” once I had achieved specific goals. Such a proposition floored me. She’s now my wife of 11 years. Okay, I’m kidding. I don’t even remember her name.

My trainer was a hustler. I didn’t sleep with her. Not because she wasn’t attractive, and it wasn’t a great motivator, but because that’s not how I do business, and that’s because I am NOT a hustler.

A hustler will do anything to get something. Hustlers flirt to get sales. Hustlers post half-naked pictures on social media to get you to buy their products. Hustlers are the algae eaters of the business world. And listen, some of their tactics work. But if you're going to build and have a long term business, you must have an entrepreneur's mentality. Hustling will only get you so far, like a bus on a route. That bus has a set-out course that it must follow. It will only get so far. That's a hustler, a bus. An entrepreneur is a plane. With a flight plan, a little fuel, and maintenance, you can pretty much go anywhere.

What is a Hustler?

A hustler, as defined by Dictionary.com, is "an enterprising person determined to succeed. A go-getter." This is what most people mean when they say that they are a hustler. That sounds good! Ain't nothing wrong with being determined to succeed. But let's look at the other four definitions attached to this word;

"Slang. A person who employs fraudulent or unscrupulous methods to obtain money; swindler.

Informal. An expert gambler or game player who seeks out challengers, especially unsuspecting amateur ones, in order to win money from them.

Slang. a prostitute.

80% of the use of that word is attached to something negative. And this is used to describe yourselves and your business? You only mean the first part of the definition, right? I get that, and I understand that. But everything else attached to this word has a negative connotation to it.

Powerful Words

Your words have power. The Bible says so in Proverbs 18:21. Your words have life and death in them. Calling yourself a hustler is not speaking life when 80% of the word's definition means something negative. If you are going to have a thriving black-owned business, the first thing you've got to do is have the right wording. You've got to say the right stuff, the right way at the right time.

Now, as you may know, I don't like the word hustler when it comes to business. But using the right words isn't just about how you describe your business or yourself as a business owner. You need to use the right words in everything you do. The right words in a contract can save you thousands of dollars and hours of court battles. Your marketing's right words can attract repeat customers that will support your business for years to come. The right words open doors that wrong words close.

You don't sell products; you offer goods and services. You don't run a business out of your house; you're a mobile business or online-based company (no matter what you do, you need an online presence). You're not a hustler; you're an entrepreneur. Do you see how that works?

Wording matters.

You are an entrepreneur, a founder; a CEO; a BLACK CEO; a boss—all of those great words you could use to describe yourself in business rather than hustler. Think about how you feel calling yourself a hustler versus how you think calling yourself a CEO.

An entrepreneur is "a person who organizes and manages any enterprise, especially a business, usually with considerable initiative and risk. An employer of productive labor; contractor." See the difference? One word has prostitute attached to it. The other word has enterprise attached to it. Which one do you want your business ascribed to?

Why Wording Matters

I occasionally get into fights with people on social media. I know you've never seen that before, but yeah, it happens. One of the conflicts that I've gotten into more recently is the debate over defunding the police. Most people simply want to reappropriate some funds towards community initiatives. But the word defund means to take away all funds from them. I have a problem with that.

The wording was defended by some people on social media, saying that it may seem misleading, but it makes you do your research. Upon doing your research, you will see that by defunding, they mean diverting funds to other projects rather than police. My response was simple, “then why not use the word DIVERTING funds?”

Someone said it's just semantics. Is it, though? Any campaign slogan I have to research to see whether I can support it isn’t a good campaign slogan. People need to know what you mean by the words you say when you say them. If this book’s motto were “Defund White Businesses,” you would think I want to take all money from businesses owned by white people. If the slogan is, “Spend Black,” then you’d know what I was talking about immediately. You’d know that I mean for you to spend your money with black-owned businesses.

Slogans (and any marketing for that matter) should be simple, memorable, and straightforward.

We'll talk more about this in the marketing chapter, but you must understand that some will always misconstrue the words you use to describe your business or products, but it shouldn't be misunderstood by many. It will be misunderstood by many if you use words that make you feel some kind of way, but others don't feel the same way. Clear communication is necessary for any successful relationship, especially the one between you and your customers.

So up your word game. Use a thesaurus sometimes. Think a little harder before you say that phrase or use that word. Be creative, have fun, and be clear and concise. You must win your customer in 7 seconds. The right words matter if you're going to do that.

Here's a word game to help you understand the need for the use of the right words. You are selling products, and when you offer those products for a lower than the regular price, your products are "on sale." But your products can also be for sale without them being ON sale. If they want to add something and then they want that product, that other product too. Which means they've purchased two products from you. They want excellent customer service, and they won't settle for less. See what I did there? Proper wording matters.

You may have read the last few paragraphs and didn't agree with what I said about using the word hustler. I understand. We have been programmed for too long to think too low. Hustler is too low. That's what dealers do on the corner is a hustle. That's what beggars do. Hustling is not what you do. You are building an empire. You are making something to pass down to your kids. You are building a business, a legacy. Not a dream. Not a fantasy. A real-life, money-making, positive, and profitable business. Period.

What if I'm an Actual Hustler?

While building your business, using the right words is hard to do when doing a hustle, calling it a business. There are so many schemes out there that will have you feeling like you have a business and an owner when you're just a 1099 contractor of a multi-level marketing scheme. In which case, you are a hustler. I'm tired of seeing black people getting roped into these schemes, scamming their family & friends to support a "business" that is not changing your life, but altering your relationships for profit. These scams use fake titles like "Diamond Level Sales Genie," social media, relationship building, parties, and more to get you roped into a system. That system is not about the product; it's about getting you to buy it to sell it. We don't have time for that kind of stuff anymore. As a community, it's time to graduate from hustling to building.

I'm not against people making some side money, and the truth is some of these tactics work. But sometimes people get into doing these schemes, and they become turned off to doing business all together because they don't succeed, and all they hear are stories of people who have succeeded and made tons of money for them. It becomes discouraging when you're not doing the same.

So if you are a hustler and I've offended you, then good. That's the first step to change. Don't put this book down because you're offended, though. Still get what I have to offer here. But consider what I said you Black CEO, you. Look at you smiling.

Chapter

2

Customer Service

Chapter 2: Customer Service

Listen, I love me some black people, and I love supporting black-owned businesses, but many of us are terrible when it comes to customer service. This is the main point of this book. I decided to write it to help us with customer service. We cannot have successful businesses without excellent customer service. This will make the difference between a repeat customer and a bad review.

We aren't just wrong on the business side, but many of us are bad on the customer side too! We are not good customers to black-owned businesses. So we'll take this chapter and discuss both sides of customer service from the customer standpoint and the business standpoint.

Being A Bad Black Customer

Let's start with us as customers. We have to be more supportive and understanding when it comes to dealing with black-owned businesses. They are not Amazon or Walmart. Black businesses do not have the resources and finances of these larger competitors. They may not be able to get things as cheap as you'd like for them to be. They may not be able to offer the fastest service all the time. We have to understand that.

Some of us customers treat black businesses as hustles. Sometimes because that's how they treat their business, and I'll get on them in a minute, but we must learn how to treat black enterprises as businesses. Expecting discounts and low prices all the time is not always possible. Hoping them to have your product ready in 24 hours like Amazon Prime isn't always a possibility. As a customer, you may not know what it takes to produce that product and send it to you.

"Yeah, but Black Businesses are Expensive Sometimes."

Black Businesses often have higher prices because they don't have connections to inexpensive suppliers. If I'm Korean and open a Beauty Supply Store, I have Korean suppliers I can connect with to supply my store at a fraction of cost. If I'm black and opening a beauty supply store I may not have black suppliers to help stock my business. Furthermore, I may not have access to capital to stock my store with lower-priced items because banks lend to black businesses only 1/10 times. So I get my products where I can, paying a higher fee on the back end. I then have to charge you a higher price as my customer because I have to pay to replace that product when you buy it, have some money to add other products, pay my overhead costs (rent, utilities, employees, etc.) and make a profit to live off of. While all businesses have those challenges, it can be more challenging when I'm not working with a race-friendly supplier who is willing to offer me deep discounts because we're of the same race.

You, as a customer, may not realize why the coconut oil in the Black store is a dollar higher than the coconut oil down the street at the Korean store, but often it is the scenario I gave above.

I've personally tested this. I purchased something in Mexico for $13 that a Mexican friend of mine later purchased for $3. Because he was Mexican, spoke the language, read the menu, and saw the prices (I was told there was no menu, which I knew was a lie), he paid $10 less than I did. So if he was selling it, he could sell it for $9 ($3 to replace it, maybe $2-$3 on overhead and business investments, and a $3 profit), whereas I'd have to sell the same product for $29-$39 ($13 to replace it, $13 for overhead and business investments, $3-$13 for profit). On the surface, which one would you go to? $9 or $29? But knowing what I just told you, wouldn't you instead support the black business and just encourage them to find cheaper suppliers?

Let's take it a step further; we will then get on social media and talk about how it's a shame that the Black business charges $20 more than the Mexican one. Black businesses are climbing out of a hole that we never created, a 400-year-old hole. We are just getting started, and everyone has had a 400-year head start and never a system stacked against them. We've got to be more patient and understanding when it comes to black people and black businesses.

Because we don't have networks and connections large enough to force suppliers' hands, we as entrepreneurs are often stuck with the short end of the stick. This is why we must circulate more dollars in our communities through our black businesses. There are over a Trillion dollars of buying power in the black community, but less than a third of that is coming back to our community. We give it to everyone else. And the crazy part is they often produce our culture and sell it back to us.

One of the other things we have to stop doing as black customers is complaining about black-owned businesses. You didn't have a bad experience because a black person owned it. You had a bad experience because of poor management and customer service. I've had poor customer service from every race I've encountered. I'm sure you have too. But for some reason, we have less patience with our own. We expect them to jump through hoops for our business sometimes, and when they don't, we let the world know, "this is why I don't support black businesses."

By no means am I saying there aren't some terrible black businesses out there. I'm just saying we have to start handling them differently because there are awful White, Mexican, Korean, and every other race-businesses out there. We have to stop singling out our own.

When you experience poor customer service, speak to management. Tell them that you're unhappy and want to continue to support them. But if they won't get their stuff together, then, by all means, find another business to patronize.

One of the reasons I started OfficialBlackApp.com is to help black businesses. I just figure that those with poor customer service or slow service just don't know how to be better. I just refuse to believe that they just want to stay poor performing. So with my experience, I can do something about it. So we offer classes, money, and other opportunities to improve the quality of their businesses. I even have a customer service class that is free for black-owned businesses. Owners and their staff can watch the classes right on their phones and improve their customer service.

Now that's not just a shameless plug about my business. It's showing you how I created a business to solve a problem. I want black businesses to succeed, so I made a platform to help them do it. I won't sit and complain. I'm going to do something about it because God gave me the ability to. You can do the same by being a better customer.

Here are some tips on being a better black customer:

1. **Don't get an attitude.** I know this can be challenging at times because some cashiers act as you owe them! But please remember they are usually overworked and underpaid. Try and be more understanding, even when they are not.
2. **Speak to the manager/owner, respectfully.** You catch more flies with honey, they say.

Use honey, don't talk "ish" to managers and owners.

3. **Compliment excellent service and tell the world.** We tell thirteen people when we don't like our service. We only tell two people when we like it. Let's normalize celebrating awesome customer service.
4. **Thank a cashier who's offering excellent service.** What's celebrated is repeated.
5. **If you must complain online (I've done my share), don't complain about them being a black-owned business.** Complain about them being a poorly managed business. Be honest, but don't make it about race.

Being a Better Black Business

Alright, here is the meat and potatoes of this book. We've got to have some real honest conversation about how we manage our businesses. Some of us have an excellent vision for our company but not a great strategy. Sometimes our prices are too high because we charge what we want to make versus the product's actual worth and value. Sometimes we hire family members or friends who give poor customer service to our clients, impacting sales. Some of us started our business ignorant of certain things, and years later, we're still clueless. We must do better.

Customer Service

Let's deal with the big issue first, customer service. Our businesses often have poor customer service because we want to be treated as owners and not servants honestly.

You **are** an owner. If your cousin works for you, she should have some pride in her work because her family owns the business. She's apart of the family enterprise. Make sure she knows and understands that. If she does not, there's a college student waiting to take her place for the same pay and will listen more. Don't accept poor customer service from your employees because they're related to you. They are taking food out of YOUR mouth and money out of YOUR pocket. I'd rather have a bigger check and a mad cousin than a happy cousin and smaller check. Say Amen somebody.

Now, it's okay that there is an air about you because you're an owner, actually, you should. However, in the transaction between you and a client, you are the servant. You are serving that person a product or service. It is a privilege to have that person shopping with you. They should feel that way. That's why it's called customer SERVICE. You are serving your customer.

That doesn't mean you have to brown-nose, but it does mean you have to show appreciation. And you have to show that appreciation continuously throughout the process, from beginning to end and after.

You don't get to say you won't do certain things because it wastes your time. Like responding to certain social media posts that are clear on your flyer, post, or website. Find a way to make it so that you're not actually wasting time, but never take it out on the clients.

I had a friend that owned a business. She got on social media complaining about the things that people were doing that hurt her business. I picked up the phone and told her to remove that foolishness. You don't complain about customers to other potential customers. You're not teaching them how to treat your business; you're teaching them how immature you are. Make the necessary adjustments, pick up the phone, and complain to a friend. Putting it on social media was not smart, and she may not have realized it, but it cost her some business. I know for a fact that it did.

You are the business owner. Therefore YOU must take the risk in the transaction. I refuse to patronize a business that will take no risk but will take my money. What I mean is, you want me to take the risk of purchasing your product, giving you my money on a website I've never seen to get a product I don't know if I'll ever like, and you don't offer refunds. Why don't you have to take any risk when you're asking for my business? This kind of thinking produces poor customer service. You decided to start this business; there has to be some risk on your part.

One time I designed some shirts for a church organization. They ordered 100 shirts from me. It was my largest order to date. I would have made a $500 profit had my online printer did their job. I waited for weeks and never got the shirts. And what's worse is they told me the shirts would be ready and shipped to me just two days before the event that needed the shirts. I ordered a month in advance and never got the shirts. They claimed they were delivered and stolen. Yeah, I believed somebody stole 100 church shirts from a secured delivery location. Sure.

I fought to get my money back, but I knew it would take days, if not weeks, to get my money back for shirts that I ordered with my own money because I only made my client only put a down payment down for the shirts (my risk). So I researched for a local printer that could get these shirts made for me in one day, and I found one. But it cost me big time. It cost me double the cost of what I was selling the shirts for. So I either go back to my client and say, "my business screwed up," and give him his deposit back, or I pay out of pocket a ton of money to get the shirts delivered on time. I spent the money and got the shirts. You know why? Because the only way my customer was getting let down is if I had no other options. I found one. It cost me, but I kept my word.

Now you might think I'm crazy but let me teach you something. These 100 shirts are going to be worn at a convention with 5,000+ people in it. If I did a good job designing them, don't you think I'd get other orders from so many different people seeing my shirt design? It cost me an additional $500 (I also didn't make the $500 profit, so a total loss of $1,000), which I just chalked up to marketing costs, but my gamble paid off. I got seven other orders, which gave me a $2000 profit. I didn't lose $1,000, I invested in keeping my customer, and I got a 100% return on my investment.

I know you can't always afford those kinds of risks because money is tight, but you must have some sort of risk if you want great customers who will return and purchase from you again. If they have to take on all the risk, you're hustling them, and they're not patronizing you.

The bottom line is, answer questions. Answer questions for which you've already posted the answers. Answer dumb questions. Answer the questions you answered in your social media post. Answer questions that are posted on your website.

People do not always read, and that one on one interaction with you can make the difference between them buying or not. You can also use it as an opportunity to upsell. Interaction with customers or potential customers is never a bad idea. Are some a waste of time? Yes. That's the cost of business. Answer those questions or politely push them to where the answer is. Never just shut them down or ignore them.

On a social media site, a networking group that I am in had a post in it from a lady. She posted a screenshot of the conversation she had with a girl who's business she was trying to patronize. The conversation poster asked the business owner how much a price was for a particular item shared on her social media without a price. The business owner responded, “are you asking so you can buy,, or you’re just asking to be asking?” The poster remained an excellent customer and said, “I’m looking to purchase later this week when I get paid and wanted to plan out my money.” The business owned should’ve just answered at this point, but no, she gets even more ignorant. “Girl, please! Hit me when you are ready to buy. I ain’t got time to be answering all these questions for no money!”

The poster said the famous line that made me write this book, “that’s why I don’t support black businesses. We are too ignorant.” I cringed as I read that.

First, the post should have included prices AND a link to purchase the product. Always make it as easy as possible for people to buy.

I’ve heard it said that people wouldn’t post prices because other businesses sometimes see your price and undercut you. Yeah, that happens. It’s called competition. But you don’t run your business to try and keep away competition. You run your business so well that a competitor copies you because you’re just that doggone good. If you don’t have competition, you don’t know where to improve. If a competitor steals from you, learn from them. Customers don’t always want the lowest price. They want good service more.

Pricing

This leads me to my next point: we have to work on as business owners; pricing. In the scenario above, I talked about how your suppliers cost more because you're black or (I'll add to that) because you're small. So if you're faced with that kind of situation, you have to opt for lower profits. You can't always make what you want to make per product, but you can make what you want to make in volume. Selling ten products with a $10 profit each is $100. Selling just two products at a $20 profit is only $40. Sometimes you're pricing yourself out of the game.

Charge what the product is worth, not what it cost you to create it (in your time and effort). I know you don't want to hear that, but just because it took you 3 hours to produce doesn't mean it's worth more to me as your customer. It's worth more to

YOU for that reason. So price it right so people can buy what you're so proud of.

I wanted to support a particular business. I saw their products on social media (with no prices or website) and loved what I saw. I didn't see prices, but I went for it anyway. When they told me the cost of the product, I nearly decided against it. I went on ahead and bought it, but I'll never repurchase the product. The price of the product was double what I felt it was worth. But they felt as though their hard work made it worth more. It does not. It's a $3 product that they put $10 worth of additions to and charged way more than that for purchase. Big mistake because I'll never purchase from them again. Not because the product wasn't right or quality but because the cost was just too high.

It doesn't mean your labor means nothing. It means that you need to find a cheaper, faster way to create this product so that you can profit without marking the retail cost up so high. It's a great product, and everything about it was excellent, but the price was still too high, and I know ten other people who would've bought from them if the cost was lower. Hopefully, that business takes advantage of resources & classes we offer on our site, OfficialBlackApp.com, so they can reduce the cost and make more sales.

Pricing is one of the most critical factors in your business being successful, but it's beyond pricing. You don't have to be the cheapest, and you don't have the reputation of a well-known luxury brand to charge a lot. You need to be priced right. Do your research and look at the cost of similar products. Consider how yours is different. How's their packaging? How's their marketing? How's their social media? How can you improve and make your product look better? How can you make your marketing stronger? Are your posts getting in the way of your business on social media? We'll talk more about that in the next chapter, but all of this points to your success or your demise.

Have A Sale

One trick I will teach you is to have a sale. I know, big secret trick, right? If the cost to make your product is $10, and you are selling it for $20, then that is a 100% markup on your work. Try having a sale at $15. You just knocked 25% off your product. You market it as such, and people will see more value in your work and company. Don't sell it as $5 off. It is 25% off! Sounds better right?

Now I know you want to make more than $5 a product, so don't do this for too long. But do this while making people sign up for your email list or text message list. You're sacrificing $5, but you're gaining access to a customer who can become a repeat customer. In reality, you're not sacrificing; you're marketing. 25% off is a great marketing strategy, especially if your product costs a bit more than it should.

Make sure when you make a sale, you're not going into the red. Take into account the cost of making the product, marketing the product, and shipping. But this is a great way to test what I'm saying.

Chapter

3

Branding Your Black Business

Chapter 3: Branding Your Black Business

Your brand is who you are, plus what you say about who you are. You can't just say, "my name is," and that be your brand. You must say, "my name is... and I am," or "I do." The colors, fonts, shot angles, and pictures—literally everything you do add-to or take-away from your brand. You must know this to be a successful black-owned business because many black-owned businesses are damaging their social media brand.

I had a friend that has a reasonably successful business but would get on social media and vent about things that customers would do that she didn't like. One week she put up three posts and engaged back and forth with other clients concerning some things that people had done. I let her know that this was wrong and frankly kind of ghetto. I told her, call me, another business owner, and vent in private. You don't vent to your clients about your clients. She defended her vent and never really got what I was trying to tell her. She still does it from time to time, and I just cringe.

See, she's *relatively* successful. But I saw that she could be so much further along. But when your mindset isn't open to growth and change, you are doomed to stay the same or worse, decline. Now years later, she's in the same position. She's better positioned but still in the same place. Knowing that your brand is essential and can change your business's trajectory can take you from a "solopreneur" to a CEO. Have some people working under you.

I tried to shift her mindset because I believed in her business, but she just wouldn't budge. There was one more area she wouldn't listen to me in, and guess what? She's in the same position years later. Now, I'm not saying I have all the answers; I don't. But the ones I do have, I try and share. You have to be open to listening when it comes to your brand. It could be the difference between 12 hours days working for yourself and 12 employees working for you!

Social Media Branding

Social media is one of the most excellent tools of modern history. But many of us have become so enthralled with the attention that we get from it that we don't realize it is also damaging us, especially many business owners. What we say, how we say it, and even who we say it to impacts our brand.

Let's study 2 different real social media accounts and discuss the successes and failures of them. I won't give the names of the accounts, but both are real accounts on social media.

About six years ago, I came across the profile of this creative young lady we'll call "Diane." Diane was saved, beautiful, smart, and had a great business idea that led to her becoming well known and making over a million dollars. I was excited for her. I harbored no jealousy in my heart; I was just excited to see a young black person make it big and have some success.

Diane didn't have an excellent logo for her business. Her business name was corny, and she didn't have many followers back then. But Diane stayed consistent and persistent. She knew her looks played a part in her success, so she was always "did up" when she did a live video or took a picture. Every picture is partnered with a caption. Each caption points people to her business in some way. She did very well and didn't see the level of success she wanted. So she started engaging her audience to help her make some changes. It worked. I looked up, and she was hovering around 100,000 followers! Many of which were important figures and influencers in her niche.

She did very well and began telling others how to do as well as she did. Her business shifted to a consultant model rather than a product-based model. But that's when things started taking a turn for the worse.

Diane let the money and success go to her head. You could see it in every post and video she put up. She became financially focused rather than product and service focused. She let her brand fall to the pits, and I'm not sure if she just didn't notice or just didn't care because the money was coming in. Now she's facing court battles and being accused of being a fraud. I unfollowed her and haven't had anything to do with her in a while, but we used to message each other and encourage each other's business moves back in the day. She used to like my posts and drop encouraging words in the comments.

What lesson can we learn from Diane?

- **Don't let it go to your head.** Don't believe your hype. Be grateful, and thank God when you experience victories but don't let the wins make you think that you can quit the work that got you the wins in the first place.
- **Expect the money to come in.** That way, you're not taken aback by it when

it does. On Officialblackapp.com, we have a shirt that says, "Millionaire Before 40." I designed the shirt because I expect to be a millionaire by then. It won't surprise me when I get it because I'm working on it and expecting it. When I get it, I'll maintain the mentality of gratefulness.

- **Choose your business moves carefully.** Don't just do what works. Do the things that you are passionate about because there will come a time that it won't work for a while. Your passion will keep you pushing and improving until it does.

The next social media account I want to look at is “Brian’s.” Brian is brilliant. He has great ideas, knows how to market, and is a whiz with social media. But Brian wasn’t always like that. When he first used social media, he put up a few things that could harm his image. He is a Christian. Like many other people using social media initially (and many even now), he didn’t know how to separate what he put out from his personal life and his ministry persona. He had pictures of him hugged up with women. He had a couple of pictures with him drinking liquor and a few posts with some curse words.

After a few months, he had a revelation; he couldn't keep posting like that and expect the Christian community to continue to respect him. He had to consider this because his page was beginning to attract many "big time" and famous people in the Church. People who he wanted to work with and be respected by. Brian got smart and changed his social media profile. He deleted most of his old posts and pictures and shifted to being more spiritual.

Because I know "Brian" personally, I can tell you that he wasn't a hypocrite. He simply didn't have a safe space just to be himself. So he thought social media could be that place. He used to get in chat rooms (I bet my younger readers have no idea what that is) and create fake names and act a fool there. But in there, no one knew who he was. He was just a screen name. Social media changed that anonymity by forcing people to create profiles. Now you're not just a screen name. You're a real person.

Brian was not thinking in the beginning. He used social media in the wrong way.

My dear, beautiful black entrepreneur, are you using social media the wrong way? Does it benefit you in any way, shape, or form to have pictures up that make you look unprofessional? Based on the people you are trying to attract to your business, are you posting things that would turn that demographic away?

What can we learn from Brian?

- **Everything doesn't have to be posted**. Who are you trying to impress anyway?
- **Ensure your social media posts don't offend the demographic you're trying to attract to your business.** You can't be a Christian, running a Christian company; however, your page is full of things that would offend Christians.
- **When being personal on your social media, ask yourself if it adds to your business or takes away**. If it takes away, then take IT away. You don't have time to be social media famous but harming your business. Those days are over.

Your brand is the face of your business. You must protect it at all costs. Protect it from negative reviews. Protect it from negative comments, and protect it from even you.

Chapter

4

Points Of Success

Chapter 4: Points Of Success

- **Don’t make people inbox you for prices.** I know some of you have services that require further investigation before you can offer a price, but when marketing, you seem like you’re scheming when you can’t just provide a price. Offer a sliding price-scale like “between $10-$25 depending on certain factors.” Or offer a price right in the middle. If $10 is the lowest, and $25 is the highest, then say prices are “around $17 depending on a few factors.” Or offer the highest price and say, "$25 and below." That way, if it is lower, they will feel like they got a deal.

- **Don't complain about your customers on social media.** Get some friends you can talk to. DO NOT complain about people who are spending money or considering spending money with you. It's tacky and distasteful.
- **Your customer service needs to be par none.** You know this is the biggest complaint that people have against our businesses, and often they are right. People do not have to spend money with you. And just because they don't spend now doesn't mean they won't spend later. Treat your clients and potential clients exactly how you want to be treated.

- **Don't charge based on how hard you've worked on it.** Those socks aren't worth $50 because you bedazzled them by hand. They are socks. They are worth $10-$20 max. They are charged based on the customer's perspective, not yours.
- **Don't argue with people online.** Sometimes it's best to ignore. You need to delete their comments and move on.
- **Fail Fast.** If it's not working, don't give up; just change what's not working. If something doesn't sell, don't throw it away. It may just be the wrong time. Bringing it back later may cause it to sell then. Right now, just shift to something else and shelf what isn't working.

- **You don't want to give up. You just need rest**. Know the difference between failure fatigue and just needing rest. Mental rest is key to having a sharp mind and great ideas. Physical rest is required to have the strength to work on your business. Get your rest.
- **Network. Network. Network!** Facebook has many groups that are related to your niche and black-owned businesses. Join them and network. Support others. Ask for others to support you.
- **Ask for support.** Don't be afraid to ask friends and family to support your business. Ask strangers too.
- **Have a friends and family discount**. I know we tell people who are our friends and family

not to ask for discounts. Listen, they're going to. You avoid the risk of them asking for too much by offering the discount upfront. Larger brands have friends and family discounts. Why shouldn't we? And trust me, you'll feel a lot better if they are supporting you even with a deal. Just ask for them to market your brand online. Now you can chalk the discount up to marketing.

- **Be your billboard.** You should be wearing your products as much as possible. If you are service-based, then create shirts that push your business. Visit OfficialBlackApp.com for shirts you can customize for your business.

- **You don't have to be perfect**. Just do it. Just go ahead. Don't be bootleg, but you don't have to be perfect. Go for it. Do your thing.
- **You still need business cards.** I know this seems crazy because we don't use business cards like that anymore. But if you do in-person events, you need cards. You can use small 4 x 6 flyers instead, but you need something to hand someone else. Now don't get 5,000, but 250 or so should be good to have on hand. Make sure to include social media info on them.
- **Keep going.** God put this idea in you. Following it will give you the life you desire to live.

Here are some tools to use for your business:

Canva (graphics)

Bit.ly (link shortener)

Picsart (edit photos)

Magisto (make movies, commercials)

hAPPyAppsBuilder.com (build apps for your business)

Google Drive (write blogs, create press releases, write books)

Thanks for reading. Make your black-owned business succeed.

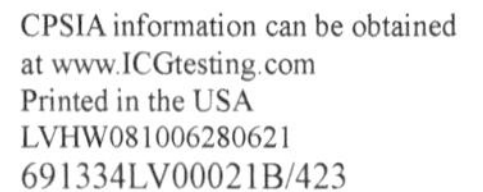

CPSIA information can be obtained
at www.ICGtesting.com
Printed in the USA
LVHW081006280621
691334LV00021B/423